Ocean Vuong is the author of the critically acclaimed poetry collection *Night Sky with Exit Wounds* and the *New York Times* bestselling novel *On Earth We're Briefly Gorgeous*. A recipient of the 2019 MacArthur "Genius Grant," he is also the winner of the Whiting Award and the T. S. Eliot Prize. His writings have been featured in *The Atlantic*, *Harper's Magazine*, *The New Yorker*, *The New York Times*, and elsewhere. Born in Saigon, Vietnam, he currently lives in Northampton, Massachusetts.

Praise for *Time Is a Mother*

"Written in the aftermath of his mother's death, Vuong's poems are raw with grief and darkness, but there are radical moments of joy and resilience even through that. Through these poems, Vuong sings loud and clear of everything worth living for and discovering." —NPR (Books We Love)

"[A] stirring collection of poetry. [Vuong] experiments with language and form while probing the aftermath of his mother's death and his determination to survive it. Take your time with these poems, and return to them often." —*The Washington Post*

"There's something about Vuong's writing that demands all of your lungs.... These ghost poems are about the cavernous corners of loss, grief, abandonment, trauma, and war, but that doesn't result in nihilism or apathy for life; in fact, Vuong approaches death like an entrance rather than an ending." —*The Guardian*

"Tender and heartbreaking . . . This collection of poems thoughtfully considers grief, both as an emotion and a sacred act, revisiting the history he shared with his mother and the understanding of family they forged together. . . . Vuong traverses the intensely personal and the broadly political with grace and courage."   —*Time*

"It's a body of work as hauntingly beautiful as it is ultimately hopeful, and very possibly Vuong's best yet."   —Vogue.com

"Piercing . . . The poems in *Time Is a Mother* give us a path to examine the complexities of what it means to lose a mother. . . . In Vuong's tender yet unflinching words, we are reminded that only a mother can carry a beating heart within her body."
                                                —*Los Angeles Review of Books*

"Like Orpheus descending into the underworld, Vuong takes us to the white-hot limits of his grief, writing with visionary fervor about love, agony, and time. . . . Aesthetically ambitious and ferociously original . . . Here, he breaks open and rebuilds."   —*Esquire*

"That's the essence of Vuong's talent: he alchemizes deeply individual experiences with universal emotions into what is both familiar and new. . . . We need no more proof of Vuong's importance in the poetic canon."   —*Chicago Review of Books*

"These poems glisten and rattle. . . . Vuong expertly unwraps clichés and rewraps them in fresh packaging so we can perceive their meanings anew. . . . His poems say, We're all humans having human experiences. Let's figure this all out together."   —*Vulture*

"Ocean Vuong's *Time Is a Mother* is haunting, inconsolable, and at the same time a playful, generous in spirit, tender, inimitable book. The poet's late mother is these pages' muse and guardian spirit, as poem after poem Vuong redefines our idea of what an elegy can do, what it is *for*. But from all of this intersection of tragedy and tenderness, true wisdom comes: Vuong teaches us not just how to grieve, but how to live."
                                        —Ilya Kaminsky, author of *Deaf Republic*
                                                        and *Dancing in Odessa*

TIME IS A MOTHER

Ocean Vuong

PENGUIN BOOKS

THỜI GIAN LÀ MỘT NGƯỜI MẸ

PENGUIN BOOKS
An imprint of Penguin Random House LLC
penguinrandomhouse.com

First published in the United States of America by Penguin Press,
an imprint of Penguin Random House LLC, 2022
Published in Penguin Books 2023

ISBN 9780593300251 (paperback)

THE LIBRARY OF CONGRESS HAS CATALOGED
THE HARDCOVER EDITION AS FOLLOWS:

Names: Vuong, Ocean, 1988– author.
Title: Time is a mother / Ocean Vuong.
Description: New York : Penguin Press, 2022.
Identifiers: LCCN 2021031789 (print) | LCCN 2021031790 (ebook) |
ISBN 9780593300237 (hardcover) | ISBN 9780593300244 (ebook)
Subjects: LCGFT: Poetry.
Classification: LCC PS3622.U96 T56 2022 (print) |
LCC PS3622.U96 (ebook) | DDC 811/.6—dc23
LC record available at https://lccn.loc.gov/2021031789
LC ebook record available at https://lccn.loc.gov/2021031790

Printed in the United States of America
1   3   5   7   9   10   8   6   4   2

BOOK DESIGN BY LUCIA BERNARD

for Peter

&

for my mother, Lê Kim Hồng, called forward

Forgive me, Lord: I've died so little!

—*César Vallejo*

Contents

The Bull

He stood alone in the backyard, so dark
the night purpled around him.
I had no choice. I opened the door
& stepped out. Wind
in the branches. He watched me with kerosene
-blue eyes. *What do you want?* I asked, forgetting I had
no language. He kept breathing,
to stay alive. I was a boy—
which meant I was a murderer
of my childhood. & like all murderers, my god
was stillness. My god, he was still
there. Like something prayed for
by a man with no mouth. The green-blue lamp
swirled in its socket. I didn't
want him. I didn't want him to
be beautiful—but needing beauty
to be more than hurt gentle
enough to want, I
reached for him. I reached—not the bull—
but the depths. Not an answer but
an entrance the shape of
an animal. Like me.

Snow Theory

This is the best day ever
I haven't killed a thing since 2006
The darkness out there, wet as a newborn
I dog-eared the book & immediately
Thought of masturbation
How else do we return to ourselves but to fold
The page so it points to the good part
Another country burning on TV
What we'll always have is something we lost
In the snow, the dry outline of my mother
Promise me you won't vanish again, I said
She lay there awhile, thinking it over
One by one the houses turned off their lights
I lay down over her outline, to keep her true
Together we made an angel
It looked like something being destroyed in a blizzard
I haven't killed a thing since

Dear Peter

        they treat me well
here they don't
        make me forget
the world like you
        promised but oh well
I'm back inside
        my head
where it's safe
        cause I'm not
there the xanax
        dissolves & I'm
okay this bed
        no longer stranded
at sea the door
        coming closer
now & I'm gonna
        dock some days
I make it to
        the reading room
they have one flew over
        the cuckoo's nest can you
believe it but hey
        I think I'm getting better
though I learned

in the courtyard yesterday
I'm still afraid
of butterflies
how they move so much
like a heart
on fire I know it doesn't
make sense this pill
a bone-shard of will
unwilling me Peter
I feel sorry
for anyone
who has to die despite
the fact I was
fifteen once but
who knows I tell lies
to keep from
falling away
from me you
wouldn't
believe it a man
in the back of
a walgreens once said
I can make you look
like something true

fuck he said
oh fuck you're so much
                like my little brother
so I let him kiss me
                for nothing oh well
childhood
                is only a cage
that widens
                like this sunlight honest
through the clinic window
                where a girl
on methadone
                claps alone
at a beige butterfly
                knocking its head up
the beige wall Peter
                I'm wearing your sea-green socks
to stay close I swear
                I'll learn to swim
when I'm out once
                & for all
the body floats
                for a reason maybe
we can swim right up

to it grab on
kick us back
to shore Peter I think
I'm doing it right
now finally maybe
I'm winning even
if it just looks like
my fingers are shaking

Skinny Dipping

some boys
        have ghosted
from this high

but I wanna go
        down on you
anyway to leap

from the bridge
        I've made
of my wrongs look

they lied to us
        no one here
was ever ugly look

if you see
        me then
I prayed

correctly I leapt
        from the verb
taking off

my best shirt
       this rag & rage
a tulip too late

in summer's teeth
       like the blade
in a guillotine I won't

pick a side
       my name a past
tense where I left

my hands
       for good oh
it should be

enough to live
       & die alone
with music on

your tongue
       to jump from
anywhere & make it

home
        to be warm & full of
nothing oh

I kept my hope
        -blue Vans on
this whole time

to distract you
        from my flat ass
did it work oh

my people my people
        I thought
the fall would

kill me
        but it only
made me real

Beautiful Short Loser

Stand back, I'm a loser on a winning streak.

I got your wedding dress on backward, playing air guitar in these streets.

I taste my mouth the most & what a blessing.

The most normal things about me are my shoulders. You've been warned.

Where I'm from it's only midnight for a second
& the trees look like grandfathers laughing in the rain.

For as long as I can remember I've had a preference for mediocre bodies, including this one.

Tell me this, how come the past tense is always longer?

Is the memory of a song the shadow of a sound or is that too much?

Sometimes, when I can't sleep, I imagine Van Gogh singing Leonard Cohen's "Hallelujah" into his cut ear & feeling peace.

Green voices in the rain, green rain in the voices.

Oh no. The sadness is intensifying. How rude.

Hey [knocks on my skull], can you get me out of here?

That one time Jaxson passed out beside a triple stack of jumbo pancakes at Denny's after top surgery.

I can't believe I lost my tits, he said a minute before, smiling through tears.

The sadness in him ends in me tonight.

It ends tonight! I shouted to the cop who pulled us over for dreaming.

I'm not high, officer, I just don't believe in time.

Tomorrow, partly cloudy with a chance.

I'm done talking, sir, I'm saying what I feel.

Inside my head, the war is everywhere.

I'm on the cliff of myself & these aren't wings, they're
futures.

For as long as I can remember my body was the mayor's
nightmare.

Now I'm a beautiful short loser dancing in the green.

You think I'll need a gun where we're going?

Can you believe my uncle worked at the Colt factory for
fifteen years only to use a belt at the end?

Talk about discipline. Talk about good lord.

Maybe he saw that a small thing moving through a large
thing is more like a bird in a cage than a word in the mouth.

Nobody's free without breaking open.

I'm not sad, he told me once, laughing, *I'm just always here.*

See, officer? Magic is real—we all disappear.

Why aren't you laughing?

No, not beauty—but you & I outliving it. Which is more so.

Somehow, I got me for days. Got this late light
in the yard, leaving blood on the bone

-colored fence. This thrash of spring we drown in to stay
awhile & mean it. I mean it when I say I'm mostly

male. That I recall every follicle in the failure the way they'll
remember god after religion: alone, impossible & good.

I know. I know the room you've been crying in
is called America.

I know the door is not invented yet.

Finally, after years, I'm now a professional loser.

I'm crushing it in losses. I'm mopping the floor
where Jaxson's drain bags leaked on his way to bed.

I'm done talking, officer, I'm dancing

in the rain with a wedding dress & it makes sense.

Because my uncle decided to leave this world, intact.

Because taking a piece of my friend away from him
made him more whole.

Because where I'm from the trees look like family
laughing in my head.

Because I am the last of my kind at the beginning of hope.

Because what I did with my one short beautiful life—
was lose it

on a winning streak.

Old Glory

Knock 'em dead, big guy. Go in there
guns blazing, buddy. You crushed
at the show. No, it was a blowout. No,
a massacre. Total overkill. We tore
them a new one. My son's a beast. A lady
-killer. Straight shooter, he knocked
her up. A bombshell blonde. You'll blow
them away. Let's bag the broad. Let's spit-roast
the faggot. Let's fuck his brains out.
That girl's a grenade. It was like Nam
down there. I'd still slam it though. I'd smash it
good. I'm cracking up. It's hilarious. You truly
murdered. You had me dying over here. Bro,
for real though, I'm dead.

You Guys

brushing my teeth at two
        in the morning I say
over my shoulder
        you guys you guys I'm serious
what are we going to make
        of this mess my voice
muffled with wintergreen foam what
        are we going to do now
that it hurts when I look
        at those I love like
you two you
        who have been through
so much together the thick & skin
        of it I'm proud of you both
I say as the foam pinkens
        through my lips I'm told
our blood is green but touches the world
        with endings my name a place
where I've waited for
        collisions you guys are
you listening I'm sorry
        for being useful only
in language are you still
        with me I ask as I peer into the tub

where I placed them gently down
        the two white rabbits
I'd found on Harris St the way back
        from Emily's where we watched *American Dad!*
on her mom's birthday her
        mom who would've been 56
this year we ate rocky road
        in bowls with blue tulips
I'm too tired she said
        to be this happy
& we laughed without
        moving our hands perhaps
the rabbits are lovers or sisters sometimes
        it's hard to tell gender
from breathing
        earlier I had scooped them
from the pavement
        they were crushed but only
kinda one
        had a dented half-face
the other's back flattened like
        a courage sock
I cradled them wetly
        in my sweatshirt but now

the tub is a red world save for the silent
       island of fur flickering
in my fugitive words guys I say
       just wait for me alright
just wait a bit longer I swear
       I'll leave this place spotless
when I'm done I say
       reaching back to
my wisdom teeth forgetting
       it's been four years
since they're gone

Dear Sara

What's the point of writing if you're just gonna force
a bunch of ants to cross a white desert?
—COUSIN SARA, AGE 7

& if you follow these ants
they'll lead you back to
stone tablets
an older desert
where black bones
once buried are
now words where
I wave to you
at 2:34 am they survived
the blast by becoming
shrapnel embedded in
my brain which
is called learning but maybe
I shouldn't talk
like this maybe I should start
over Sara I messed up I'm
trying to stay clean but
my hands are monsters
who believe in
magic Sara the throat is also

an inkwell black
oil wrung through
your father's fingers
after a day beneath
the Buick say
heartbreak & nothing
will shatter say Stonehenge
& watch the elephants sleep
like boulders blurred
in Serengeti rain it doesn't
have to make sense to be
real—your aunt Rose gone
two years now like
a trick they forgot
to finish & the air holds
your voice as
it holds its own
vanishing maybe *you*
are the true soldier
ant hoarder of
what's so massive
it could crush you into
a twitching
comma Sara

your name sharpens daily
against the marble
of your mother's teeth there
are sparks in every
calling & called we press
our faces to the womb
till we're jokes on
our way to cracking up & maybe
you're right little ant
queen with your shoes
the shade of dirty
paper white desert
your pink & blue pens
untouched after all
who can stare at
so many ruins & call it
reading this family
of ants fossilized
on the page you slam
the book shut look out
at the leafless trees
doused in red April rain
where none of us
are children long enough
to love it

American Legend

So I was driving
with my old man. The day wasted
save for the cobalt haze
closing around us.
We were on our way to kill
our dog, Susan. I mean, we had to
bring her to the clinic
to put her down, this
murder or maybe
they meant put her *in*
the ground—though I knew Susan
would be ashed in
the incinerator
out back. Puffs
of smoke, little ghost
poodles. Where was I going
with this? Right—the car,
the rain, the legend of joy
& pain. My old man
& I, the Ford big enough
for us to never
touch. & maybe I meant to
make the hairpin turn
too hard. & the thing flipped

like a new law, going 80. Maybe
I wanted, at last, to feel him
against me—&
it worked. As the colors spun
through the windshield, wild
metal clanking
our shoulders, the sudden
wetness warm
everywhere, he slammed
into me &
we hugged
for the first time
in decades. It was perfect
& wrong, like money
on fire. The skin
around his neck so soft, his
aftershave somehow
summer. It lasted
not a second but
he was smiling, his teeth already
half-gone, as if someone
wiped them away to make room
for something truer. Put it
down on the page, son, he said

one night, after telling me
why he did what he did
with his life, shitfaced
on Hennessy. We were sitting
at the kitchen table before his shift
at the sock factory. His eyes: raindrops
in a nightmare. I touched him, then
let go. The car stopped
rolling, we hung upside down
as things dripped. Steam
or breath. I did
what any boy would do
after getting exactly
what he wanted: I kissed
my father. He grinned
I think. His pupils
elsewhere. I reached back, unlatched
the cage. The dog
stepped out, sniffed
my old man, still warm, then ran
into the trees, into her second
future. I walked from the wreck
till the yards became
years, the dirt road

a city, until my face
became this face & the rain
washed the gasoline clean
from my fingers. I found
a payphone in the heart
of the poem & called you
collect to say all this
knowing it won't make
a difference, only
more. So hello, hi, the blood
inside my hands
is now inside
the world. Words, the prophets
tell us, destroy
nothing they can't
rebuild. I did it to hold
my father, to free
my dog. It's an old story, Mother,
anyone can tell it.

The Last Dinosaur

When they ask me what it's like, I tell them
imagine being born in a hospice
in flames. As my relatives melted, I stood
on one leg, raised my arms, shut my eyes & thought:
tree tree tree as death passed me—untouched.
I didn't know god saw in us a failed
attempt at heaven. Didn't know my eyes had three
shades of white but only one image
of my mother. She's standing under an ancient
redwood, sad that her time on earth is all
she owns. O human, I'm not mad at you for winning
but that you never wished for more. Emperor
of language, why didn't you master *No*
without forgetting *Maybe*? Sure, we can
make out if you want, but I'm warning you—
it's a lot. Sometimes I think gravity
was like: *To be brutally honest . . .* & then
never stopped talking. I guess what I mean
is that I ate the apple not because the man lied
when he said I was born of his rib
but that I wanted to fill myself with its hunger
for the ground, where the bones of my people
still dream of me. I bet the light on this page
isn't invented yet. I bet you never guessed

that my ass was once a small-town
wonder. That the triceratops went nuts
when I danced. How once, after weeks
of drought, I walked through my brother's laughter
just to feel the rain. O wind-broke wanderer, widow of hope
& ha-has. O sister, dropped seed—help me—
I was made to die but I'm here to stay.

II

Rise & Shine

Scraped the last $8.48
from the glass jar.
Your day's worth of tips

at the nail salon. Enough
for one hit. Enough
to be good

till noon but
these hands already
blurring. The money a weird

hummingbird caught
in my fingers. I take out
the carton of eggs. Crack

four yolks into a day
-white bowl, spoon
the shells. Scallions hiss

in oil. A flick
of fish sauce, garlic crushed
the way you

taught me. The pan bubbling
into a small possible
sun. I am

a decent son. Salt
& pepper. A sprig
of parsley softened

in steam. Done,
the plate fogs its own
ghosts. I draw a smiley face

on a napkin
with purple marker.
I lace my boots. It doesn't

work—so I tuck them in. Close
the back door. Gently
the birches sway but never

touch. The crickets
unhinge their jaws
in first light, last

syllables crackling
like a pipe steady
over a blue flame

as footsteps dim
down a dawn-gold road
& your face

at the window
a thumbprint left over
from whose god?

The Last Prom Queen in Antarctica

It's true I'm all talk & a French tuck
but so what. Like the wind, I ride
my own life. Neon light electric
in the wet part of roadkill
on the street where I cut my teeth
on the good sin. I want to
take care of our planet
because I need a beautiful
graveyard. It's true I'm not a writer
but a faucet underwater. When the flood comes
I'll raise my hand so they know
who to shoot. The sky flashes. The sea
yearns. I myself
am hell. Everyone's here. Sometimes
I go to parties just to dangle my feet
out of high windows, among people.
This boy crying in his car
after his shift at McDonald's
on Easter Sunday. The way
he wipes his eyes with his shirt
as the big trucks blare
off the interstate. My favorite
kind of darkness is the one
inside us, I want to tell him.

&: I like the way your apron
makes it look like you're ready
for war. I too am ready for war.
Given another chance, I'd pick the life
where I play the piano
in a room with no roof. Broken keys, Bach
sonata like footsteps fast
down the stairs as
my father chases my mother
through New England's endless
leaves. Maybe I saw a boy
in a black apron crying in a Nissan
the size of a monster's coffin & knew
I could never be straight. Maybe,
like you, I was one of those people
who loves the world most
when I'm rock-bottom in my fast car
going nowhere.

Dear T

on my desk this field of snow
where you're lying too still
          all I have to do is write
                    the right words & I'm

beside you (again) but
          all these letters &

                    nothing
               says your face—fashioned
                    from nouns muscular
               inflection bones

hardened with the
alphabet's reduction see? a flick
          of my wrist & a house rises
                    from the snow

a wide porch—like you wanted—
          sunflowers in the front yard

                         late afternoon light
               on the latticed apple pie

                    a bed with cloud-white blankets
            & a fireplace that won't

        look—a bit of ink on the pad
& we're running down the street again
                after the thunderstorm
                        platelets still plenty

            in veins beneath your cheek: green branches
            in a sunset sky which is almost

                            impossible—is too much
                    so I scratch it out I make laughter
                            instead make a song
                    on the radio that erupts

        into static the moment I enter
your throat opening
                into *Whoa* but
                        let me spell out

        these m-a-p-l-e-s just right
                so we'll have a few more seconds

                              in the shade
                    look you say *the trees*
                              are falling they're being
                    axed down

          pressed into white fields or
tax forms or discharge papers or
                    you won't stop coughing up blood
                              maybe

          we should go home now you say *my father*
                    will kill me I haven't told my father

                              I'm on it
                              I'm on it all
                              it's all
                              over now stay

          a little longer I say but your voice
is already pieces
                    your grin peeling off
                              in dusted sheets & I saw

this coming: each night the pen gets so far
       & runs out of

               nights you write the letter dear you
            & it doesn't work so you write the poem
               but the birds are
            just holes in the gunshot

sky oh man the aubade
left to rot into afternoon
        when every word

     was forgotten as soon as the hand moved
          across the page away

              from the car crash
            but we deserve more than this you said *this*
                 is only the beginning each night
            the same snowfields

    crushed & littered across the room
maybe I can build a boy

out of the silences inside maybe
we can cease without dying fuck
without tears falling

into the truck stop urinal
& we're just too tired
to walk home we're
just two boys lying

in the snow &
you're smiling because the stars
are just stars & you know

we'll only live once
this time

Waterline

If I should wake & the Ark
the Ark already
gone

If there was one shivering thing
at my side

If the snow in his hair
was all that was left

of the fire

If we ran through the orchard
with our mouths
wide open

& still too small
for amen

If I nationed myself
in the shadow
of a colossal wave

If only to hold on
by opening—
by kingdom come

give me this one
eighth day
let me enter
this nearly-gone *yes*

the way death enters
anything—fully
& without a trace

Not Even

Hey.

I used to be a fag now I'm a checkbox.

The pen tip jabbed in my back, I feel the mark of progress.

I will not dance alone in the municipal graveyard at midnight, blasting sad songs on my phone, for nothing.

I promise you, I was here. I felt things that made death so large it was indistinguishable from air—and I went on destroying inside it like wind in a storm.

The way Lil Peep says *I'll be back in the mornin'* when you know how it ends.

The way I kept dancing when the song was over, because it freed me.

The way the streetlight blinks twice, before waking up for its night shift, like we do.

The way we look up and whisper *Sorry* to each other, the boy and I, when there's teeth.

When there's always teeth, on purpose.

When I threw myself into gravity and made it work. Ha.

I made it out by the skin of my griefs.

I used to be a fag now I'm lit. Ha.

Once, at a party set on a rooftop in Brooklyn for an "artsy vibe," a young woman said, sipping her drink, *You're so lucky. You're gay plus you get to write about war and stuff. I'm just white.* [Pause] *I got nothing.* [Laughter, glasses clinking]

Because everyone knows yellow pain, pressed into American letters, turns to gold.

Our sorrow Midas touched. Napalm with a rainbow afterglow.

Unlike feelings, blood gets realer when you feel it.

I'm trying to be real but it costs too much.

They say the earth spins and that's why we fall but everyone knows it's the music.

It's been proven difficult to dance to machine-gun fire.

Still, my people made a rhythm this way. A way.

My people, so still, in the photographs, as corpses.

My failure was that I got used to it. I looked at us, mangled under the *Time* photographer's shadow, and stopped thinking, *get up, get up.*

I saw the graveyard steam in the pinkish dawn and knew the dead were still breathing. Ha.

If they come for me, take me out.

What if it wasn't the crash that made us, but the debris?

What if it was meant this way: the mother, the lexicon, the line of cocaine on the mohawked boy's collarbone in an East Village sublet in 2007?

What's wrong with me, Doc? There must be a pill for this.

Because the fairy tales were right. You'll need sorcery to make it out of here.

Long ago, in another life, on an Amtrak through Iowa, I saw, for a few blurred seconds, a man standing in the middle of a field of winter grass, hands at his sides, back to me, all of him stopped there save for his hair scraped by low wind.

When the countryside resumed its wash of gray wheat, tractors, gutted barns, black sycamores in herdless pastures, I started to cry. I put my copy of Didion's *The White Album* down and folded a new dark around my head.

The woman beside me stroked my back, saying, in a midwestern accent that wobbled with tenderness, *Go on son. You get that out now. No shame in breakin' open. You get that out and I'll fetch us some tea.* Which made me lose it even more.

She came back with Lipton in paper cups, her eyes nowhere blue and there. She was silent all the way to Missoula, where she got off and said, patting my knee, *God is good. God is good.*

I can say it was gorgeous now, my harm, because it belonged to no one else.

To be a dam for damage. My shittyness will not enter the world, I thought, and quickly became my own hero.

Do you know how many hours I've wasted watching straight boys play video games?

Enough.

Time is a mother.

Lest we forget, a morgue is also a community center.

In my language, the one I recall now only by closing my eyes, the word for *love* is *Yêu.*

And the word for *weakness* is *Yếu.*

How you say what you mean changes what you say.

Some call this prayer, I call it watch your mouth.

Rose, I whispered as they zipped my mother in her body bag, *get out of there.*

Your plants are dying.

Enough is enough.

Time is a motherfucker, I said to the gravestones, alive, absurd.

Body, doorway that you are, be more than what I'll pass through.

Stillness. That's what it was.

The man in the field in the red sweater, he was so still he became, somehow, more true, like a knife wound in a landscape painting.

Like him, I caved.

I caved and decided it will be joy from now on. Then everything opened. The lights blazed around me into a white weather

and I was lifted, wet and bloody, out of my mother, into the world, screaming

and enough.

Amazon History of a Former Nail Salon Worker

Mar.

Advil (ibuprofen), 4 pack
Sally Hansen Pink Nail Polish, 6 pack
Clorox Bleach, industrial size
Diane hair pins, 4 pack
Seafoam handheld mirror
"I Love New York" T-shirt, white, small

Apr.

Nongshim Ramen Noodle Bowl, 24 pack
Cotton Balls, 100 count
"Thank You For Your Loyalty" cards, 30 count
Toluene POR-15 40404 Solvent, 1 quart
UV LED Nail Lamp
Cuticle Oil, value pack
Clear Acrylic Nail Tips, 500 count

May

Advil (ibuprofen), 4 pack
Vicks VapoRub, twin pack
Portable Electric Nail Drill

Salonpas Heat-Activated muscle patch, 40 count
Lipstick, "Night Out Red"
Little Debbie Chocolate Zebra Cakes, 4 boxes

Jun.

Large faux-clay planter pots, value set
Carnation Condensed Milk, 6 pack
Clear Nail Art Acrylic Liquid Powder Dish Bowl, 2 pcs
Birthday Card—Son—Pop-up Mother and Son effect
Nike Elite Basketball Shorts, men's small

Jul.

Saviland Holographic Gold Nail Powder, 6 colors
Nescafé Taster's Choice Instant Coffee
Advil (ibuprofen), 4 pack
PIXNOR Pedicure Double-Sided Callus Remover
Bengay Medicated Cream, 3 pack

Aug.

Newchic Ochre Summer Dress Floral Print, sz 6
Wrigley's Doublemint Gum, 8 pack
Plastic Adirondack Lawn Chair, colonial blue

Sep.

Nail buffers and files, 10 pcs
Coppertone Sunblock, 6 oz

Oct.

CozyNites Fleece Blanket, pink
Sleep-Ease Melatonin caps, 90 count
Icy Hot Maximum Strength pain relief pads

Nov.

Tampax, 24 count
Faux-Resin Hair clips, 3 pack

Dec.

Advil (ibuprofen) Maximum Strength, 4 pack
True-Gro Tulip Bulbs, 24 pcs

Jan.

Feb.

Healthline Compact Trigger Release Folding Walker
Yankee Candle, Midsummer's Night, large jar

Mar.

Chemo-Glam cotton head scarf, sunrise pink
White Socks, women's small, 12 pack

Apr.

Chemo-Glam cotton scarf, flower garden print
"Warrior Mom" Breast Cancer awareness T-shirt, pink and
    white

May

Mueller 255 Lumbar Support Back Brace

Jun.

Birthday Card—"Son, We Will Always Be Together,"
    Snoopy design

Jul.

Eternity Aluminum Urn, Dove and Rose engraved, small
Perfect Memories picture frame, 8 x 11 in, black
Burt's Bees lip balm, Honey, 1 pc

Aug.

Sep.

Easy-Grow Windowsill herb garden

Oct.

YourStory Customized Memorial Plaque, 10 x 8 x 4 in
Winter coat, navy blue, x-small

Nov.

Wool socks, grey, 1 pair

Nothing

We are shoveling snow, this man and I, our backs coming closer along the drive. It's so quiet every flake on my coat has a life. I used to cry in a genre no one read. What a joke, they said, on fire. There's no money in it, son, they shouted, smoke from their mouths. But ghosts say funny things when they're family. This man and I, we take what will vanish anyway and move it aside, making space. There is so much room in a person there should be more of us in here. Traveler who is inches away but never here, are you warm where you are? Are you *you* where you are? Something must come of this. In one of the rooms in the house the man and I share, a loaf of rye is rising out of itself, growing lighter as it takes up more of the world. In humans, we call this *Aging*. In bread, we call it *Proof*. We're in our thirties now and I rolled the dough just an hour ago, pushing my glasses up my nose with a flour-dusted palm as I read, reread, the hand-scrawled recipe given me by the man's grandmother, the one who, fleeing Stalin, bought a ticket from Vilnius to Dresden without thinking it would stop, it so happened, in Auschwitz (it was a town after all), where she and her brother were asked to get off by soldiers who whispered, *keep moving, keep moving*, like boys leading horses through wheat fields in the night. How she passed the huddled coats, how some were herded down barbed-wire lanes. The smoke from our mouths rising as the man and I bend and lift, in silence, the morning clear as one inside a snow globe. How can we know, with a house full of bread, that it's hunger, not people, that survives? He pours a bag of salt over the pavement. From where I'm standing it looks like light is spilling out of him, like the dusty sunray that found his grandmother's hands as she got back on the train, her brother at her side, smoke from the engine blown across the faces outside, which soon fall back to pine forests, washed pastures, empty houses with full rooms. The man clutches his stomach as if shot, the light floods out of him—I mean you. Because something must come of this. When the guard asked your grandmother if she was Jewish, she shook her head, half-lying, then took from her bag a roll, baked the night before, tucked it in the guard's chest pocket. She didn't look back as the train carried her, newly twenty, toward where I now stand, on a Sunday in Florence, Massachusetts, squinting at her faded scrawl: *sift flour, then beat eggs until happy-yellow.* The train will reach Dresden days before the sky is filled with firebombers. More smoke. A bullet or shrapnel, failing to find her. The brother under rubble, his name everywhere around her like the snow falling on your face forty years later, on December 2, 1984, while your mother carries you, alive only three hours, the few steps to the minivan where your grandmother, sixty now, crowns your head with her brother's name. *Peter*, she says, *Peter*, as if the dead could be called back into new, stunned bones. The snow has started up again, whitening the path as though nothing happened. But to live like a bullet, to touch people with such intention. To be born going one way, toward everything alive. To walk into the world you never asked for and choose a place where your wanting ends—which part of war do we owe this knowledge? It's warm in this house where we will die, you and I. Let the stanza be one room, then. Let it be big enough for everyone, even the ghosts rising now from this bread we tear open to see what we've made of each other. I know, we've been growing further apart, unhappy but half full. That clearing snow and baking bread will not fix this. I know, too, as I reach across the table to brush the leftover ice from your beard, that it's already water. *It's nothing*, you say, laughing for the first time in weeks. *It's really nothing.* And I believe you. I shouldn't, but I do.

Scavengers

                    Your body wakes
into its quiet rattle
                         Ropes & ropes
          How quickly the animal
empties
          We're alone again
                    with spent mouths

Two trout gasping
                         on a June shore
Side by side, I see
                    what I came for, behind

your iris: a tiny mirror
                              I stare
into its silver syllable
                    where a fish with my face
twitches once
          then gones

                    The fisherman
                         suddenly a boy
with too much to carry

III

Künstlerroman

After walking forever through it all, I make it to the end.

The REWIND button flashes red __ red __ red.

I sit down and push the button. The screen flicks on,
revealing a man in a pressed black suit sitting at the edge of
a dirt road, staring into a Panasonic TV set from the '80s.

I watch him rise and walk backward, down the unmarked
road, past the gutted mobile homes, empty concrete slabs
crisscrossed with weeds, then through a pine grove littered
with dead needles, which soon opens to a field of poppies,
past a ravine choked with cars rusting from another century.

He walks backward through the night-green hills, hands
in his pockets as the crescent moon, an empty boat, skims
the sky.

He walks backward into town, up the steps of the grand
hotel, into a hall crowded with crystal chandeliers, waiters
with plates of caviar spoons, flutes of champagne. The room
a kingdom of light.

The man is surrounded by merry people in fine dress. They whirl backward around him, faces flushed with opulence. The tie he wears (too big) is the one his cousin, Victor, gave him outside of Drew's package store, saying "You're a writer now, you should look like one" three weeks before Victor checked himself into the psych ward at Silver Hill.

One by one the people hand the man a book, the artifact of his thinking. He opens each one and, pen in hand, traces a deliberately affected, illegible signature, until the name, in red ink, evaporates. Everyone raises their glasses, satisfied, mouths open as crickets start up around me, the screen flickering as the tape whirs.

I watch him walk backward through the crowd, alcohol flowing through their lips into glasses as he leaves the hall toward the empty streets, alone.

He walks as the sun rises, then falls, through days, weeks, then months.

He walks backward through airports, convention centers, dips into taxis, even a limousine, then a governor's mansion, through immaculate foyers of leather-embroidered divans and marble mantels, Tiffany lamps, polished granite counters, rooms just for "sitting" where no one ever sat. Fresh fruit piled in teak bowls set to rot.

The tape skips and I see, on the screen, a sheet of dust shoot up from the surface of a river, then gather into a cloud under a bridge, before funneling into the copper urn cradled in the man's arms.

His face looks unfinished. The man's little brother rests his head on the man's shoulder. In their oversize rented suits, they look like ambassadors from a country that no longer exists.

It is the country of sons.

//

I watch him leave another mansion in reverse, down a long driveway flanked with phlox and geraniums, down a mountain road at night, through towns whose names you hear only when a hurricane passes through, gas stations overgrown with ragweed and asters, past an alley wide as a gravestone, over gravel medians where somebody's sister was last captured on CCTV. I see him walk backward into a row house with eight satellite dishes jammed on the garage roof. The dark of a basement. The sound of needle wrappers torn open, the occasional face from high school, thirty-twoed and sucked out under a two-second match.

A voice bashed against a wall turns to dust in his cochlea as the warmth of junk passes through him like a new spine. He can feel their laughter in his hands.

Cigarettes spark in the dark: fireflies in a bomb shelter.

He walks backward past the cornfield (where, at seven, he lost his dog, Cheetah, and sat for two hours in the corn crying) and picks up his suit jacket hung on a broken hydrant. He puts it on and continues backward toward his mother's house, where he kisses her on the cheek in a grimy kitchen, the $50 bill going from his hand to hers, then back into her bra. He heads up the stairs, into the bathroom, and lets the vomit in the sink rise to his mouth. Snot back up his nose. Hands shaking.

//

The tape skips—I see him lying on the floor in a dimly lit room, eyes shut, the dark wetness at his starched collar drying back to tears, the tears crawling up his cheeks.

He blows his nose, rises to his knees, hands over his face. A framed medal, an ornate award, slides into his arms. He kisses it, searches the glass for his face, then gets up, flicks on the lights.

He's in a dressing room, surrounded by mirrors. His red, wet eyes on every wall.

He walks backward through double doors, shafts of light, the award tucked under his arm. Through a foyer, down a wide linoleum hall, reporters flanking him, cameras, forced grins, stiff handshakes, half hugs, then he backs onto the wing of a stage in the baroque opera house. The crowd roars mutely, the award raised with both arms, its gold edges glimmering under clinical houselights. His heart a fish tossed into the wooden boat inside him.

The tape skips and I see him go backward out of the Stop & Shop in Hartford, the one that starts to crumble, brick by brick, as he gets further away. Bulldozers, men in hard hats—until it's razed to the ground, then replaced by larger, irregular stones, until it becomes the walls of a century-old church, the steeple rising under the wrecking ball's touch. Pieces of stained glass gather into Saint Francis's haloed face.

He walks backward into the church, where Kelvin's casket glows in the dusky light. Mothers and grandmas with heads bowed. But what he wants, or rather, what I want for him, doesn't happen: underneath Kelvin's button-up, the stitched pink eye in his chest, just above his right lung, doesn't open, the .45-caliber shell doesn't come out, won't suspend itself in Sunday's air, won't make an obedient return to the barrel, splinter into lead, polymer, iron, elements, the ash of a star ejected from a cosmos into this one.

Kelvin doesn't sit up in his casket to kiss his father, Mr. Rios, on the forehead when the man hobbles back to take the Tonka truck from his nineteen-year-old boy's hands.

//

The dictator on TV, the noose removed from his neck as the world watches. The dictator crawling backward into the hole in the ground, his face a crumpled law.

I keep my finger on REWIND, like a good citizen, and the man in the suit keeps running backward through the narrative—that is, the knowledge—I've forced on him.

Summer approaches spring as he walks backward, freshly eighteen, into a motel room off Route 4, where his clothes come off like bandages. Where he lies very still on the lumpy bed beside a soldier, just back from the desert, where he left his right ear. The light from the street falls into the hollow where the ear once was, making a medallion of gold on the side of the man's head. The boy runs his tongue across it and waits to be forgiven.

On the wall, the shadows of their erections fall, then rise. We are rare in goodness, and rarer still in joy. Their clothes return to them, like crumpled laws.

He walks backward as the soldier walks backward. They smile at each other until both are out of sight. The night returns to itself, less whole. The Maybelle Auto marquee a beacon in the fog.

//

And the tanks roll out of Iraq, the women backing away from their dead, rags over their mouths.

Books disintegrate to trees as the tape roll thins. The trees rise to their feet. The drugs leave the veins of four friends in the Mazda, the car flipping nine times on I-84 and landing on its wheels, their necks re-boned to their lives as they sing Ja Rule and Ashanti's "Mesmerize," eyes shut in a freshman high.

The boy sitting at a desktop computer as, one by one, the words, often accompanied by unsolicited dick pics, vanish from AOL Chat screens.

asl? stats?
are you a virgin?
can you meet now?
are you down?
are you Asian or are you normal?
can I be your dad for an hour?
do you know how 2 love yet?
i can get a room
u can do ur homework while i work on that ass
are you there?
hey i won't hurt you

call me
faggot
I need you
fuck you

All of it draining back into binary code.

Then the gypsum, calcite, plaster, and lead particles rise from the pavement in massive billowing clouds, and the North Tower reconstructs itself and September's clear and blue again, and the people float up, arms open, to stand looking out of windows in good suits, in good bones.

And the dahlias raise their heads, their chins high along the courthouse lawn.

//

The tape scrambles and I see the boy dancing with his mother in the front yard in the '97 nor'easter, snow floating back up the sky as he twirls under her shadow—cast larger than life by sodium lights. The flakes going up to thicken god's pillow for his never-ending sleep.

The ice retreats, the ground beneath him red and ochre as if an enormous mammal had been opened at his feet. And the leaves rush in the gusts, attach themselves, by thousands, to oak branches across the yard. His mother, at the window, lifts her head from her hands, eyes drying.

I see the boy walk backward into his house, ease his mother down on the kitchen tiles. His father's fist retracts from her nose, whose shape realigns like a fixed glitch. If I slowed it down here, I might mistake the man's knuckles for a caress, as if soothing something with the back of his hand so it won't fall apart.

//

The cake on the table, air returning to the boy's pursed lips as the seven candles, one by one, begin to light, and the wish returns to his head where it's truer for never being touched by language.

I am starting to root for him, on his way to dust.

//

The tape skips to the family howling, ecstatic on the front lawn, their arms waving in a summer night. The son, clutching his stuffed Elmo, runs in circles as they all head inside, where the mother picks up the phone: she's gotten a job at the clock factory in Meriden.

The Hubble telescope swoops the other way. Halley's Comet shoots back behind the trees as the Humvees roll, again, into Iraq.

He walks backward past an empty carnival where a tobacco field had greened a few months back. It's the day after the Tri-County Fair, I can tell, where all that remains of October are sunken pumpkins along the road to the city jail, and the clowns sweating on stools behind their trailers wiping away makeup in pie-tin mirrors.

The cornfield husked and rattling in the breeze, the highway beyond the pines with its air of gasoline and burned rubber. He walks backward—though there's so little time left to destroy. Backward until he bowls over, on his hands and knees. Until he's crawling on his belly almost like a soldier with a missing ear, his grey Champion hoodie browning in blotches, until soot appears on his cheeks and neck. His jeans fall away in crisp pieces as he drags himself down the road where he made his name. A thin line of blood lights along his jaw.

I press PAUSE here but nothing stops because my hands are his hands.

And all that's left are his tattered boxers as he crawls backward, half-naked, arms covered in cuts, toward the smoke rising from the ditch by Risley Road.

When he gets there, he slips his feet through the Mazda's mangled rear window, fastens the seat belt, turns his head toward the shattered window and waits for the glass to reassemble, for the friends in the front seat to sing again, here at the end.

Reasons for Staying

October leaves coming down, as if called.

Morning fog through the wildrye beyond the train tracks.

A cigarette. A good sweater. On the sagging porch. While the family sleeps.

That I woke at all & the hawk up there thought nothing of its wings.

That I snuck onto the page while the guards were shitfaced on codeine.

That I read my books by the light of riotfire.

That my best words came farthest from myself & it's awesome.

That you can blow a man & your voice speaks through his voice.

Like Jonah through the whale.

Because a blade of brown rye, multiplied by thousands, makes a purple field.

Because this mess I made I made with love.

Because they came into my life, these ghosts, like something poured.

Because crying, believe it or not, did wonders.

Because my uncle never killed himself—but simply died, on purpose.

Because I made a promise.

That the McDonald's arch, glimpsed from the 2 am rehab window off Chestnut, was enough.

That mercy is small but the earth is smaller.

Summer rain hitting Peter's bare shoulders.

The *ptptptptptptpt* of it.

Because I stopped apologizing into visibility.

Because this body is my last address.

Because right now, just before morning, when
     it's blood-blue & the terror incumbent.

Because the sound of bike spokes heading home at dawn
     was unbearable.

Because the hills keep burning in California.

Through red smoke, singing. Through the singing, a way
     out.

Because only music rhymes with music.

The words I've yet to use: timothy grass, jeffrey pine,
celloing, cocksure, light-lusty, midnight-green, gentled,
water-thin, lord (as verb), russet, pewter, lobotomy.

The night's worth of dust on his upper lip.

Barnjoy on the cusp of winter.

The broken piano under a bridge in Windsor that sounds
like footsteps when you play it.

The Sharpied sign outside the foreclosed house:
SEEKING CAT FRIEND. PLEASE KNOCK FOR KAYLA.

The train whistle heard through an opened window after a
nightmare.

My mother, standing at the mirror, putting on blush before
heading to chemo.

Sleeping in the back seat, leaving the town that broke me,
whole.

Early snow falling from a clear, blushed sky.

As if called.

IV

Ars Poetica as the Maker

And God saw the light and it was good.
   —GENESIS 1:4

Because the butterfly's yellow wing
                 flickering in black mud
was a word
       stranded by its language.
Because no one else
           was coming—& I ran
out of reasons.
                 So I gathered fistfuls
of ash, dark as ink,
          hammered them
                into marrow, into
a skull thick
         enough to keep
       the gentle curse
of dreams. Yes, I aimed
            for mercy—
but came only close
         as building a cage
around the heart. Shutters
              over the eyes. Yes,
          I gave it hands

despite knowing

        that to stretch that clay slab

    into five blades of light,

           I would go

too far. Because I, too,

          needed a place

to hold me. So I dipped

           my fingers back

into the fire, pried open

        the lower face

    until the wound widened

into a throat,

        until every leaf shook silver

             with that god

-awful scream

        & I was done.

& it was human.

Toy Boat

for Tamir Rice

yellow plastic
black sea

eye-shaped shard
on a darkened map

no shores now
to arrive—or
depart
no wind but
this waiting which
moves you

as if the seconds
could be entered
& never left

toy boat—oarless
each wave
a green lamp
outlasted

toy boat
toy leaf dropped
from a toy tree
waiting

waiting
as if the sp-
arrows
thinning above you
are not
already pierced
by their names

The Punctum

According to the Smithsonian, from 1830 to 1935,
there were over 350 poorly documented lynchings
in California, the victims being mostly of Mexican,
Chinese, and Native American descent.

There is sunlight here, golden enough to take to the bank. There are daffodils and sweetgrass. We have made this for you with our hands. Look at our hands, they say. There is nothing to hide. But you look closer and see, in the photo, a shadow staining the ground, over the sepia flowers, attached to no one. A hole in the dirt. And you wonder if it's an entrance or maybe the mark of something higher, something already leaving, on wings. Yes, it's just a bird, they say. A smudge of flight, defects in the camera. A product of its time. This is all a product of the times. Look at the sunlight, they say. How it falls right through. Some things are hidden in plain sight. Look, there was so much space back then. And you do look. You look and you look and it's true. There is so much air to be answered for. But your eyes return to the one black moon fallen on the ground. Life-size period unspoken for. How faithful the memory of a shadow, you think. How you can almost see the author of its curve. Now, if you could please look directly above you, they say. There is still the sky. Blue as the single eye pressed down on us. There is nothing to hide under all this sun. And your hand moves to your throat, to make sure you are still the speaker, that English is still your reckoned wreck. That it hasn't pooled into an ink-dark puddle at your feet. You feel for your throat because history has proven the skull lodged in the gravedigger's hands is often the one behind your face. But these are marigolds, they say. And these the horses. We have retouched them for your viewing pleasure. We have touched and retouched. Now, if you would come this way, they say, there is so much more to see.

Tell Me Something Good

You are standing in the minefield again.
Someone who is dead now

told you it is where you will learn
to dance. Snow on your lips like a salted

cut, you leap between your deaths, black as god's
periods. Your arms cleaving

the wind. You are something made, then made
to survive—which means you are somebody's son.

Which means if you open your eyes, you'll be back in
that house, under a blanket printed with yellow sailboats.

Your mother's boyfriend, bald head ringed with red
hair, a planet on fire, kneeling

by your bed again. Air of whiskey & crushed
Oreos. Snow falling through the window: ash returned

from a failed fable. His spilled-ink hand
on your chest. & you keep dancing inside the minefield—

motionless. The curtains fluttering. Honeyed light
beneath the door. His breath. His wet blue face: earth

spinning in no one's orbit. & you want someone to say
  Hey . . . Hey,
I think your dancing is gorgeous. A two-step to die for,

darling. You want someone to say all this
is long ago. That one night, very soon, you'll pack a bag

with your favorite paperback & your mother's .45,
that the surest shelter was always the thoughts

above your head. That it's fair—it has to be—
how our hands hurt us, then give us

the world. How you can love the world
until there's nothing left to love

but yourself. Then you can stop.
Then you can walk away—back into the fog

-walled minefield, where the vein in your neck adores you
to zero. You can walk away. You can be nothing

& still breathing. Believe me.

No One Knows the Way to Heaven

but we keep walking anyway.

        When you get here it will be different
but we'll use the same words.

        You will look & look—& see only
the world. Well, here's

        the world, small
& large as a father.

        I am not
yet your father. I tried

        to speak this morning
but the voice only went far

        as my fingers. Can you see it
now?
For the first time in weeks

        I saw my reflection in the
cup of coffee

        & kept drinking anyway.
Strange, what a face can do

        to a face. Like once,
I let a man spit in my mouth

        because my eyes wouldn't water
after Evan shot himself

        in his sister's chicken coop.
The chickens long

gone. Like him, I had been

looking for a sound to change

the light in the room.

But all I could find

was a man. His bright spit. I

lifted

my tongue as he stood

above me.

My jaw a ransacked

drawer.

I said *Please*,

because I'm a cold man

who believes every bit

of warmth should be saved

& savored. It's alright—

no one can punish us

now. Not even

the speaker.

I am wrong often—but not enough

to forget you. You

who are not yet born. Who will

always be what remains

after I build my Ark

out of everything

I lost.
Because when a man & a man

                                walk hand in hand into a bar
the joke's on us.

                    Because when a man & a man make
love, they make

                        only love. There's enough
for you, but not enough
for *you*. You indistinguishable

                           from rain. Rain: to give
something a name
just to watch it fall. What

                          will I name you?
Are you a boy or a girl

         or a translation of crushed water? It doesn't
matter. Maybe extinction

                           is temporary. Rain as it
touches ground.

                     Hey, maybe I'm right here.
Your dad

                  is right here. I'll leave the rest
of this blank

        & when you get here, I'll tell you

everything. When

       you get here, I'll show you

this incredible thing

          we can do to mirrors

just by standing still.

Almost Human

It's been a long time since my body.
Unbearable, I put it down
on the earth the way my old man
rolled dice. It's been a long time since
time. But I had weight back there. Had substance
& sinew, damage you could see
by looking between your hands & hearing
blood. It was called reading, they told me,
too late. But too late. I red. I made a killing
in language & was surrounded
by ghosts. I used my arsenal
of defunct verbs & broke
into a library of second chances,
the ER. Where they bandaged
my head, even as the black letters
kept seeping through,
like this. Back there, I couldn't
get the boys to look at me
even in my best jean jacket.
It was 2006 or 1865 or .327.
What a time to be alive! they said,
this time louder, more assault rifles.
Did I tell you? I come from a people of sculptors
whose masterpiece was rubble. We

tried. Indecent, tongue-tied, bowl-cut & diabetic,
I had a feeling. The floorboards creaked
as I wept motionless by the rehab window.
If words, as they claimed, had no weight
in our world, why did we keep
sinking, Doctor—I mean
Lord—why did the water swallow
our almost human hands
as we sang? Like this.

Dear Rose

I have known the body of my mother, sick and then dying.
—ROLAND BARTHES

Let me begin again now
that you're gone Ma
if you're reading this then you survived
your life into this one if
you're reading this
then the bullet doesn't know us
yet but I know Ma you can't
read napalm fallen on your

schoolhouse at six & that
was it they say a word
is only what it
signifies that's how I know
the arrowhead in my
back means I'm finally
pretty a word like bullet
hovers in an amber

afternoon on its way to
meaning the book opens like
a door but the only one you

ever read was a coffin its
hinges swung shut on lush descriptions
of a brother I point to
you to me today a Thursday I
took a long walk alone it

didn't work kept stopping
to touch my shadow just in case
feeling is the only truth
& there down
there between thumb & forefinger
an ant racing in circles then zigzags
I wanted significance but think
it was just the load he was bearing

that unhinged him: another ant
curled & cold lifted on
his shoulders they looked like a set
of quotations missing speech it's said
they can carry over 5,000 times their mass
but it's often bread crumbs
not brothers that get carried
home but going too far

is to admit the day ends anywhere
but here no no Mom this
is your name I say pointing
to Hồng on the birth certificate thin
as dust Hồng I say which means
rose I place your finger on a flower so
familiar it feels synthetic red
plastic petals dewed with glue I leave

it out of my poems I turn from
its face—clichéd oversize
head frayed at the edges
like something ruptured
by a bullet I was born
because you were starving but
how can anything be
found with only two hands

with only two hands you dumped
a garbage bag of anchovies into the glass jar
the day was harmless a breeze hovering
in amber light above us gray
New England branches swayed without
touching to make fish sauce you said

you must bear the scent of corpses
salted & crushed a year in a jar tall

as a boy they dropped with slick
thumps like bullets each word must stop
somewhere—why not a yellow
poet I put in the fish sauce I take out
the fish sauce I dance
on the line until I am the line
they cross or cross
out they nearly killed me

you said for being white
with a toilet plunger you pushed the fish
down sound of bones like gravel
the violet vein on your wrist glistened
your father was a white soldier
I had amber hair you said they called me
traitor called me ghost
girl they smeared my face with cow shit

at the market to make me brown
like you & your father the eyes glared
from inside the jar they shot

my brother you said looking down
but away from the dead
eyes my little brother
if reading is to live
in two worlds at once why

is he not here Ben said you can do
anything in a poem
so I stepped right out of it into
this one to be entered is
to be redefined the bullet achieves its name
by pushing flesh into flesh I was struck
by these words we say I was caught by
this passage it moved right through opened

me up these eyes reading not
yet healed shut but full of lead
-en meaning which parts
a red sea inside me sinew dusted to soft tissue
my blood a borderless translation
of errors in the reader's
hands a gaping rose Hồng
I say which also means

pink the shade every bullet meets
before finding its truest self Calvino said
human instinct is to laugh
when someone falls the soldiers
were cracking up as they fired
your brother running his sky
-blue shirt pink on the ground
our evolution as hunters Calvino went on

the collapsed body a signal
of meat thus hunger leads to lethal
joy it's almost perfect
you smiled your nose deep
in the jar because the bullet
makes you real by making you less
which is perfect in poems the text
amplified by murder

-ous deletions leads to inevitable
art the pristine prisoner
in his marble coffin the length
of a fish a timeline
across the page to document days

the dead a measurement of
living distance
the corpse blooming

as it decays Pink Rose Hồng Mom
are you reading this dear
reader are you my mom yet
I cannot find her without you this
place I've made you can't
enter within months their meat
will melt into brown mucus rot almost
-sauce the linear fish-spine dissolved

by time at last pungent scent
of ghosts you said you named me
after a body of water 'cause
it's the largest thing you knew
after god I stare at the silvered layers
the shadowed line between two pressed fish
is a finger in the dark gently remembered
in the dark his finger

on my lips Ma his shhh
your friend the man watching me

while you worked the late
shift in the Timex clock factory why
am I thinking this now the gasped throats
mottled pocked fins gently the door its blade
of amber light widening as it opened
shhh it sounds like an animal

being drowned as you churned
the jar your yellow-white arms pink
fish guts foaming up gently you must
remember gently the man he's in
the '90s still his face a black rose
closing do you know
what it's like my boy my
boy you said sweating above the jar

to be the only one hated the only
one the white enemy of your own
country your own
face the trees they were roaring
above us red leaves leaving little cuts
in the sky gently I touched
your elbow the fish swirling
in their gone merry-go-round

sightless eyes no no Ma I said
holding my breath I don't know
what it's like & turned
my head up toward the sun
which brightly cancels
if you're reading this then
I survived my life into yours
you who told your brother you were hungry

so he stole a roasted chicken
so he tucked it under his sky
-blue shirt & it's not
your fault reader you had
to work you had to get up
in the blood-blue dawn to warm
up your car you who held
instant coffee with both hands

ate your lunch of Wonder Bread dipped
in condensed milk in the parking lot
alone you bought me pencils reader I could
not speak so I wrote myself into
silence where I stood waiting for you Ma
to read me do you read me now do you

copy mayday mayday you who dreamed
of dipping shreds of chicken

into fish sauce as you hid in the caves
above your village you white
devil girl starving ghost
but I shouldn't have been so
hungry you said looking up
at the leaves vermilion through the brother
-blue sky I hated my hunger the veins
on your fists the jar all amber crush

empty as a word
-less mind stop writing
about your mother they said
but I can never take out
the rose it blooms back as my own
pink mouth how
can I tell you this when you're always
to the right of meaning

as it pushes you further into white
space how can I say the hole
in your brother's back is not

a part of your brother but your brother
aparted who is still somewhere
running because I wrote it
in the present tense the bullet held
just behind his death an insect

trapped in amber the charred
chicken clutched to his chest dust
rising from sandals
as he sprints toward the future
where you're waiting by the rain
-warped window wet footsteps
on Risley Rd but dear reader
it's only your son coming home

again after school after
the bullies put his face in brown
dirt what if I said the fastest
finger pointing to you Ma
is me would you look away
I point to you no no I went right
through you left a pink rose blazing
in the middle of the hospital

in Sài Gòn reader who
cannot read
or write you wrote a son
into the world with no
words but a syllable so much
like a bullet its heat fills you
today a Thursday
(ours not Vallejo's) partly

cloudy a little wind I
kneel to write
our names on the sidewalk
& wait for the letters to
signal a future an
arrow pointing to a way
out I stare & stare
until it grows too dark to

read the ant & his brother long
home by now night
flooding the concrete black
my arms dim as incomplete
sentences reader I've

plagiarized my life
to give you the best
of me & these words these

insects anchovies
bullets salvaged & exiled
by art Ma my art these
corpses I lay
side by side on
the page to tell you
our present tense
was not too late

Woodworking at the End of the World

In a field, after everything, a streetlamp
shining on a patch of grass.

Having just come back to life, I lay down under its warmth
& waited for a way.

That's when the boy appeared, lying next to me.

He was wearing a Ninja Turtles t-shirt
from another era, the colors faraway.

I recognized his eyes: black buttons salvaged from the coat
I used to cover my mother's face, at the end.

Why do you exist? I wanted to know.

I felt the crickets around us but couldn't hear them.

A chapel on the last day of war.

That's how quiet he was.

The town I had walked from was small & American.

If I stayed on my knees, it would keep all my secrets.

When we heard the woodcutters coming closer, destroying
the past to build the future, the boy started to cry.

But the voice, the voice that came out
was an old man's.

I reached into my pocket
but the gun was gone.

I must've dropped it while burying my language
farther up the road.

It's okay, the boy said at last. *I forgive you.*

Then he kissed me as if returning a porcelain shard
to my cheek.

Shaking, I turned to him. I turned
& found, crumpled on the grass, the faded red shirt.

I put it over my face & stayed very still—like my mother
at the end.

Then it came to me, my life. I remembered my life
the way an ax handle, mid-swing, remembers the tree.

& I was free.

Notes & Acknowledgments

The epigraph on page ix is from César Vallejo's "Agape." *The Black Heralds*, Lima Penitentiary printing press, 1919. Translated by Rebecca Seiferle, Copper Canyon Press, 2003.

In "The Last Dinosaur" the configuration "How once, after weeks of drought" is borrowed from Eduardo C. Corral's poem, *"Our Completion: Oil on Wood: Tino Rodríguez: 1999."*

"The Last Prom Queen in Antarctica": The lines "The sky flashes. The sea / yearns" and "I myself / am hell. Everyone's here" are lifted and altered from John Berryman and Robert Lowell, respectively.

"Not Even" refers to a line from Lil Peep's "Star Shopping."

"The Punctum" was inspired by artist Ken Gonzales-Day's *Erased Lynchings* series: Ken Gonzales-Day, *Erased Lynchings*, 2006, fifteen inkjet prints, Smithsonian American Art Museum, museum purchase through the Luisita L. and Franz H. Denghausen Endowment, 2012.12.2A-O, © 2006, Ken Gonzales-Day.

"Dear Rose": The epigraph is from Roland Barthes's *Mourning Diary*, translated by Richard Howard, Farrar, Straus & Giroux, 2012.

Deep gratitude to the following journals, in which some of these poems first appeared, sometimes in different forms and titles: *The Adroit Journal, The Believer, Boston Review, Brick, Freeman's, Granta, Harper's Magazine, INQUE, jubilat, The Kenyon Review, Narrative, The New Yorker, The New York Times, The Paris Review, Poetry, Poetry Northwest*, Poets.org, and *The Yale Review*.

An early version of "Dear T" first appeared in *No* (YesYes Books, 2013), a limited-edition chapbook, now out of print.

Thanks to the MacArthur Foundation and the United States Artist Fellowship for generous time and support. And to the Emily Dickinson Museum, who kindly offered time to write in Dickinson's room, where "Nothing" was first drafted.

To the perennial ships in the night who helped make this book possible and ushered these poems toward their strongest versions, thank you: Peter Bienkowski, Frances Coady, Eduardo C. Corral, Laura Cresté, Peter Gizzi, Ann Godoff, Ben Lerner, Meghan O'Rourke, Jiyun Yun, and the ace team at Penguin.